Scott Co.

Coin Chart Manual

supplementary to Thompson's Bank note and commercial reporter,

containing facsimiles of all the gold and silver coins found in circulation

Scott Co.

Coin Chart Manual

supplementary to Thompson's Bank note and commercial reporter, containing facsimiles of all the gold and silver coins found in circulation

ISBN/EAN: 9783337122461

Printed in Europe, USA, Canada, Australia, Japan

Cover: Foto ©Suzi / pixelio.de

More available books at **www.hansebooks.com**

THE

Coin Chart Manual,

SUPPLEMENTARY TO

THOMPSON'S

Bank Note and Commercial Reporter,

CONTAINING FAC SIMILES OF ALL THE

GOLD AND SILVER COINS

FOUND IN CIRCULATION,

THROUGHOUT THE WORLD, WITH THE INTRINSIC VALUE OF EACH.

FORTY-FIRST YEAR OF PUBLICATION.

THOROUGHLY REVISED AND BROUGHT UP TO THE DAY OF GOING TO PRESS.

NEW YORK:

PUBLISHED BY SCOTT & CO.,

146 FULTON STREET.

VALUE OF U. S. DOLLAR.

Abyssinia	1 Pataka or 23 Harfs.
Annam	1 Kwan 5 Mas.
Arabia	1 Piaster 16 Caveers.
Argentine Republic	1 Peso Fuerte.
Austria	2 Florins 7¼ Kreutzers.
Belgium	5 Francs 18¼ Centimes.
Bogota	1 Peso 3⅝ Centavos.
Bolivia	1 Boliviano 3⅝ Centavos.
Brazil	1 Milreis 834⅔ Reis.
Burmah	1 Bat 2 Salungs 1 Fuang 80 Kowries.
Central America	1 Peso 7 Centavos.
Chili	1 Peso 9⅝ Centavos.
China	6 Mace 2 Candareens 1 Cash.
Costa Rica	1 Peso 7 Centavos.
Denmark	3 Kroner 71 Öres.
Ecuador	1 Peso 7 Centavos.
Egypt	20 Piasters 4½ Paras.
France	5 Francs 18¼ Centimes.
German Empire	4 Marks 20¼ Pfennige.
Great Britain	4 Shillings 1½ Pence.
Greece	5 Drachms 18¼ Leptas.
Guatemala	1 Peso 7 Centavos.
Hayti	1 Dollar 5 Cents (Specie).
Honduras	1 Peso 7 Centavos.
India	2 Rupees 4 Annas ¼ Pie.
Italy	5 Lire 18¼ Centessimos.
Japan	1 Yen.
Liberia	1 Dollar.
Malta	2 Scudi 6 Tarins
Mexico	1 Dollar or Peso.
Moldavia	5 Lei 18¼ Ben Paras.
Netherland	2 Florins 10 Stivers.
Norway	3 Kroner 73 Öres.
Paraguay	1 Peso Fuerte.
Persia	4 Kwan 7½ Shahi.
Peru	1 Sol 7 Centavos.
Portugal	926 Reis.
Roumania	5 Lei 18¼ Ben Paras.
Russia	1 Rouble 33⅝ Kopecks.
Servia	5 Dinars 18¼ Paras (18¼).
Siam	1 Tical 2 Salungs, 1 Fuang and 89 Kowries.
Spain	5 Pesetas 18¼ Centimos.
Switzerland	5 Francs 18¼ Centimes or Rappen.
Tripoli	1 Mahbub 3 Piasters or 70 Aspers.
Tunis	8 Piasters 7¼ Caroubs.
Turkey	23 Piasters 25¼ Aspers.
United States of Colombia	1 Peso 7 Centavos.
Uruguay	1 Patacon or Peso and 5 1/12 Centavos.
Venezuela	1 Peso 7 Centavos.
Zanzibar	1 Janierio Dollar.

PREFACE.

We trust no apology is needed in presenting the FORTY-NINTH EDITION OF THOMPSON'S COIN CHART MANUAL to the public. We therefore call our patrons' attention to the special features of this edition. The values have been carefully revised and in several cases altered, great care being taken to give the official quotations for all the new pieces inserted. To facilitate reference an index has been added, and all the gold coins colored yellow, which will be found very convenient for brokers and others making rapid reference. We have received communications from several brokers, stating that the values of the pieces have been overrated. In reply, we would remind them that we do not profess to quote the prices they are to pay, but give the intrinsic value of coins of full weight of the designs given, the values being taken from assays conducted at the U. S. Mint. In regard to foreign gold we quote the prices which ought to be realized in U. S. gold coin, if sent to the Mint for coinage.

Persons wishing to sell a few pieces of any of the silver coins here represented can only realize about eighty for uncurrent and ninety per cent. for current coins, of the prices quoted. This reduction is owing partly to short weight, caused by the attrition to which the coins have been subjected in circulation, and the consequent loss, the balance being the charges on the transaction.

We shall be specially obliged to brokers and others who may favor us with specimens of *newly issued* foreign gold or silver coins, for which a fair per centage over their market value will be cheerfully paid.

As much counterfeit silver is now found, we annex the government test for silver coin ; it can be put up by any chemist for a few cents: 24 grains nitric silver in crystals ; 1 gramme or 15 grains of nitric acid and 1 ounce water. Remove a little of the surface of the coin with a knife and touch the place with a drop from the stopper. If good, no action ; if bad it will blacken.

Many brokers may not be aware that the following U. S. coins, on account of their scarcity, command a considerable premium, varying according to their state of preservation. Our publishers will always pay from 25 to 500 per cent. over the face value for those contained in the following list :

DOLLARS. 1794, 1796, 1804, 1798 reverse of '97, 1801, 1836, 1838, 1839, 1850, 1851, 1852, 1853, 1854, 1855, 1856, 1857, 1858.

HALF DOLLARS. 1794, 1796, 1797, 1801, 1802, 1815, 1836 like 1837, 1852.

QUARTER DOLLARS. 1796, 1804, 1823, 1827.

TWENTY CENT PIECES. 1877, 1878.

DIMES. 1796, 1797, 1798, 1800, 1801, 1802, 1803, 1804, 1809, 1811, 1822, 1824.

HALF DIMES. 1794, 1795, 1796, 1797, 1800, 1801, 1802, 1803, 1805.

THREE CENTS, SILVER. 1863, 1864, 1865, 1866, 1867, 1868, 1869, 1870, 1871, 1872, 1873.

COPPER CENTS. 1793, 1796, 1799, 1804, 1806, 1809, 1811, 1813.

NICKEL CENTS. 1856.

HALF CENT. 1793, 1796, 1802, 1811. Ten cents each will be paid for the following, 1794, 1795, 1797, 1800.

Communications to the editor should be addressed to him, care of SCOTT & CO., 146 Fulton Street, New York City.

INDEX.

THE
COIN CHART MANUAL.

CONTAINING FAC-SIMILES OF ALL THE

GOLD AND SILVER COINS

FOUND IN CIRCULATION THROUGHOUT THE WORLD, WITH THE INTRINSIC VALUE OF EACH.

FORTY-FIRST YEAR OF PUBLICATION.

THOROUGHLY REVISED AND CORRECTED, AND BROUGHT UP TO THE DAY OF GOING TO PRESS.

Published by SCOTT & CO., 146 Fulton Street, New York.

UNITED STATES.

GOLD.

Half Eagle. $5.15.   Old Eagle. $10.30.   Half Eagle. $5.15.

Double Eagle. $20.00.

Eagle. $10.00.   Half Eagle. $5.00.

$3.00.   Quarter Eagle. $2.50. $1.00.

UNITED STATES.

SILVER.

Dollar. $1.00.

Dollar. $1.00.

Dollar. $1.00.

Dollar. $1.00.

UNITED STATES. (Silver Continued.)

Trade Dollar. $1.00.

Half Dollar.   50c.

Half Dollar.   50c.

Half Dollar.   50c

Half Dollar.   50c.

THE COIN CHART MANUAL.
PLATE IV.

UNITED STATES.
SILVER.

Half Dollar. 50c.

Quarter Dollar. 25c.

Quarter Dollar. 25c.

Quarter Dollar. 25c.

Quarter Dollar. 25c.

Quarter Dollar. 25c.

Twenty Cent Piece. 20c.

Dime. 10c.

Dime. 10c.

Dime. 10c

Dime. 10c.

UNITED STATES.

SILVER.

Dime. 10c.   Half Dime. 5c.

Half Dime. 5c.   Half Dime. 5c.   Half Dime. 5c.

Half Dime. 5c.   Three Cent Piece. 3c.   Three Cent Piece. 3c.

Pine Tree Shilling. 17c.   New England Six Pence. 8c.

GOLD.

 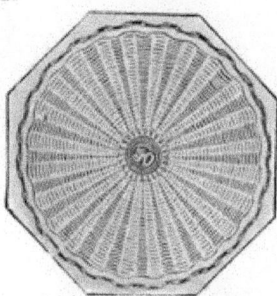

California Quintuple Eagle. $47.50

Georgia $2.39. North Carolina 1.00.   Five Dollars. $4.75.

GREAT BRITAIN.

GOLD.

Five Sovereigns. $24.30.

Sovereign. $4.86.   Sovereign. $4.86.   Guinea. $5.12.   Guinea. $5.12.

Sovereign. $4.86.   Sovereign. $4.86.

¼ Guinea 1.70.   ½ Sovereign 2.43.   ½ Sovereign 2.43.   ½ Guinea 2.56.   ½ Guinea 2.56.

GREAT BRITAIN.
SILVER.

40 Shillings. 54c.

Half Crown. 55c.

Crown. $1.10.

Crown. $1 15

Crown. 1.15.

Crown. 1.15.

2 Pence. 4c.

4 Pence. 7c.

1 Penny. 2c.

3 Pence. 5c.

4 Pence. 8c.

Crown. $1.10.

Six Pence. 11c.

Dollar. $1.05.

Shilling. 23c.

Shilling. 23c.

Shilling. 23c.

GREAT BRITAIN.
SILVER.

Half Crown. 57c.   Half Crown. 57c.

Half Crown. 57c.   Shilling. 23c.

Shilling. 23c.   Shilling. 23c.

Six Pence. 11c.   Shilling. 23c.   Shilling. 23c.   Shilling. 23c.

1½ Pence. 3c.   2 Pence. 4c.   3 Pence. 5c.   3 Pence. 5c.   4 Pence. 7c.

Token. 24c.   Token. 10c.   Token. 5c.   Token. 6c.

BRITISH COLONIES.

GOLD.

Mohur. $7.10.　　　Mohur. $7.08.　　　⅓ Mohur, $2.36.　　　Two Dollars. $2.00.

SILVER.

Rupee. 46c.　　　2 Annas. 5c.　　　　　　Half Rupee 23c.

⅛ Dollar. 11c.　　　1/16 Dollar. 5c.　　　¼ Gilder. 6c.　　　⅛ Gilder. 3c.

5 Cents. 5c.　　　10 Cents. 10c.　　　20 Cents. 20c.

Dollar. 80c.　　　　　　3 Gilders. 75c.

MEXICO. (GOLD.)

½ Doubloon. $7.76.   Ten Pesos. $9.81.

¼ Pistole. 97c.   2½ Pesos. $2.45.   5 Pesos. $4.90.

SILVER.

Dollar. $1.03.

Dollar. $1.00.   Dollar. $1.05.

Half Dollar. 53c.   Peso. $1.06.

MEXICO.
SILVER.

Peso. $1 05

¼ Dollar. 25c.   ¼ Dollar. 25c.   Real. 12c.   Real. 12c.

½ Real. 6c.   ¼ Real. 3c.   ½ Real. 6c.

GOLD.

Twenty Pesos. $19 51.

Doubloon. $15 52.

CENTRAL AND SOUTH AMERICA.
GOLD.

Doubloon. $15.60.

Doubloon. $15.53.

½ Doubloon. $7.75.   Pistole. $3.50.   Pistole. $3.75.   Pistole. $3.75.

½ Pistole. $1.87. ½ Pistole. $1.87. ¼ Pistole. 90c. ¼ Pistole. 90c. ¼ Pistole. 90. ¼ Pistole. 87c.

Four Escudos. $7.55.   Half Doubloon. $7.25.

CENTRAL AND SOUTH AMERICA.

SILVER

Eight Reals. 98c.

Eight Reals. 98c.

Eight Reals. 98c.

Eight Reals. 65c.

Eight Reals. 98c.

Eight-Reals. 65c.

Eight Reals, 98c.

Eight Reals. 98c.

Four Reals 49c.

CENTRAL AND SOUTH AMERICA.
SILVER.

½ Real. 6c.   ½ Real. 6c.   ¼ Real. 6.   Real. 12c.   Real. 12c.

Real. 8c.   Real. 12c.   Real. 12c.

Real. 12.   Real. 12c.   Real. 12c.   Real. 12c.   Real. 12c.

Real. 12c.   Real. 12c.   Real. 12c.   Real. 6c.

Half Dollar. 50c.   Quarter Dollar. 25c.

One Peso. 96c.   Dollar. 95c.

CHILI.

GOLD.

Onza, $15.50.

Pistole, $3.87.

SILVER.

Pistole, $3.87.

Eight Reals. $1.06.

Two Reals. 22c.

Eight Reals. $1.06.

Two Reals, 24c.

Peso. 98c.

Half Real, 6c.

PERU.

GOLD.

Doubloon $15.47   Pistole. $3.86.

SILVER.

Eight Reals. $1.06.   Four Reals. 38c.

½ Real. 6c.   Eight Reals. 94c.   ¼ Real. 3c.

½ Real. 6c.   Eight Reals. 94c.   One Real. 12c.

BRAZIL AND PORTUGAL.

GOLD.

Crown. $5.77.　　$1.75.　　90c.　　50c.　　50c.　　50c.

Moidore. $4.75.　　Crown. $5.77.　　Moidore. $4.75.

SILVER.

Cruzado. 50c.　　960 Reis. $1.00.

960 Reis. $1.00.　　300 Reis. 28c.

80 Reis. 12c.　　160 Reis. 24c.　　40 Reis. 6c.

BRAZIL AND PORTUGAL.
SILVER.

40 Reis. 6c.　　　　　　40 Reis. 6c.

640 Reis. 65c.　　　　　　500 Reis. 49c.

960 Reis. $1.00.

960 Reis. $1.00.　　　　　　1200 Reis. 1.00.

Milreis. 54c.

SPAIN. (GOLD.)

¼ Pistole. $1.00. Pistole. $4.00. Doubloon. $16.00. ½ Pistole. $2.00 ¾ Pistole. $1.00.

Four Piasters. $3.90 ½ Pistole. $2.00.

SILVER.

Dollar. $1.00.

Dollar. $1.00.

Dollar. $1.00.

Dollar. $1.00.

½ Pistareen. 9c.

½ Pistareen. 9c.

Pistareen. 20c.

½ Pistareen. 10c.

SPAIN. (SILVER.)

Dollar. $1.00.

Dollar. $1.00.

Half Dollar. 50c.

Ten Reals. 50c.

Dollar. $1.00.

Five Pesetas. 93c.

Half Dollar. 50c.

Dollar. $1.00.

Half Dollar. 50c.

¼ Dollar. 20c.

¼ Dollar. 20c.

¼ Dollar. 20c.

¼ Dollar. 20c.

Two Reals. 9c.

¼ Pistareen. 4c.

½ Pistareen. 8c.

THE COIN CHART MANUAL.
PLATE XXI.

SPAIN.

SILVER.

¼ Pistareen. 4c.

5 Pesetas. 96 c.

¼ Pistareen. 4c.

¼ Pistareen. 4c.

Five Pesetas. 95c.

¼ Pistareen. 4c.

Pistareen. 20c.

Pistareen. 20c.

Pistareen. 14c.

Twenty Reals. 98c.

Five Pesetas. 95c.

FRANCE. (GOLD.)

Louis d'or. 4.50.   40 Francs. $7.68.   Louis d'or. 4.50.

20 Francs. $3.84.   20 Francs. $3.84.   6 Francs. $1.12.   20 Francs. $3.84.   20 Francs. $3.84.

SILVER.

Crown of Louis XIIII. $1.06.

Crown. $1.06.   Crown. $1.06.

Five Francs. 98c.   5 Francs. 98c.   5 Francs. 98c.

THE COIN CHART MANUAL.

PLATE XXIII.

FRANCE. (SILVER.)

Five Francs. 98c.

Five Francs. 98c.

Five Francs. 98c.

Five Francs. 98c.

Five Francs. 98c.

Six Livres. $1.06

5 Francs. 98c.

Five Francs. 98c

¼ Crown. 25c.

½ Crown. 12c.

¼ Crown. 12c.

French Colonies. 8c.

Two Francs. 36c

Two Francs. 36c.

FRANCE.
SILVER.

¼ Franc. 4c.   ¼ Franc. 4c.   ½ Franc. 8c.   ¼ Franc. 4c.   50 centimes. 9c.   25 centimes. 4c.

⅛ Crown. 12c.   ¼ Crown. 24c.   10 Sols. 8c.   ½ Franc. 8c.

One Franc. 18c.   Two Francs. 36c.

AUSTRIA.
GOLD.

Quadruple Ducat. $9.12.

Sovereign. $6.75.

½ Sovereign. $3.37.

Ducat. $2.28.

½ Sovereign. $3.37.

½ Sovereign. $3.37.

½ Sovereign. $3.37.

Four Florins. $1.93.

Quadruple Ducat. $9.12.

Sovereign. $6.75.

SILVER.

Specie Dollar. $1.02.

20 Kreutzers. 15c.

20 Kreutzers. 15c.

Florin. 48c.

GERMANY.

GOLD.

Quintuple Ducat. $11.00.   5 Thalers $3.90.   Quintuple . Ducat. $11.00.

Twenty Marks. $4.76.   Ten Marks. $2.38.   ¼ Caroline. $1.18.

Five Thalers. $3.90.   Five Thalers. $3 90.   Five Thalers. $3.90.   Double Fred. d'or. $7.80.

Ten Thalers. $7.80.   Ten Thalers. $7.80.   Ten Thalers $7.80.   Ten Thalers. $7.80.

Five Gilders. $1.98.   ½ Caroline. $2.37.   Ducat. $2.20.   Ducat. $2.20.   Five Gilders $1.98.

Caroline. $4.75.   Caroline. $4.75.   Ten Thalers. $7.80.   Double Fred. d'or. $7 80.

GERMANY, (GOLD.)

Ducat. $2.20.

12 Marks. $1.55.

2½ Thalers. $1.95.

Five Thalers. $3.90.

Five Thalers. $3.90.

Fred. d'or. $3.90.

Five Thalers. $3.90.

Five Thalers. $3.90.

SILVER.

6th Thaler. 10c.

Mark. 23c.

6 Kreutzers. 3c.

Thaler. 72c.

Double Gilder. 72c.

Double Gilder. 72c.

Double Gilder. 72c.

12 Grotes 10c.

6 Grotes. 5c.

Grote. 1c.

6th Thaler. 10c.

GERMANY.
SILVER.

Thaler. 65c.

Double Thaler. $1.32.

Specie Dollar 93c.

Double Thaler. $1.32.

Rix Dollar. 93c.

Florin. 36c.

Thaler. 72c.

Thaler. 72c.

Thaler. 72c.

Florin 40c.

Florin. 40c.

GERMANY. (SILVER.)

Crown. 80c.

Half Florin. 22c.

Crown. $1.00.

Crown. 80c.

Florin. 44c.

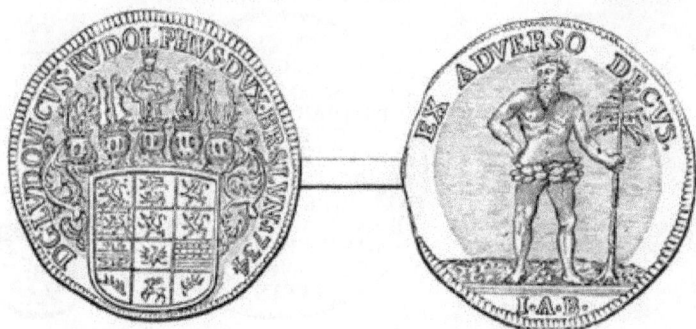

Thaler. 72c.

GERMANY.
SILVER.

30 Kreuzers 22c.

Double Thaler. $1.46.

Double Gilder. 70c.

Crown Thaler. $1.02.

Crown. $1.02.

Thaler. 93c.

Thaler. 93c.

Thaler. 93c.

Crown. $1.02.

2 Groschen. 2c.

GERMANY.

SILVER.

20 Kreutzers. 15c.

Thaler. 93c.

Florin. 44c.

Thaler. 93c.

Double Thaler. $1.32.

Thaler. 93c.

Double Thaler. $1.32.

Florin. 44c.

Thaler. 93c.

Thaler. 67c.

24th of a Thaler. 2c.

6 Pfen. 1c.

1 Schilling. 1c.

GERMANY.
SILVER

Florin. 44c.

Thaler. 93c.

Thaler. 72c.

Double Florin. 80c.

Thaler. 67c.

Florin. 44c.

12 Grote. 12c.

6th Thaler. 5c.

12 M. Groschen. 22c.

24 M. Groschen. 47c.

Thaler. 66c.

Thaler. 67c.

2½ Schilling. 3c.

1c.

½ c.

1c.

12 Grote. 10c.

GERMANY.
SILVER.

48 Schillings. $1.00

30 Kreutzer. 20c.

Thaler. 93c.

30 Kreutzers. 20c.

Rix Dollar. 93c.

1c.

2c.

12 Grotes. 5c.

1c.

1c.

Double Thaler. $1.32.

8 Skillings. 10c.

Rix Dollar. 93c.

ITALY.

GOLD.

40 Lire. $7.68.   20 Lire. $3.84.   100 Lire. $19.20.

20 Lire. $3.84.   20 Lire. $3.84.   20 Lire. $3.84.

SILVER.

5 Lire. 98c.   5 Lire. 98c.   5 Lire. 98c.

5 Lire. 98c.   2 Lire. 39c.

5 Soldi. 4c.   10 Soldi. 8c.

ITALIAN STATES.

GOLD

2 Doppia. $6.25.   96 Livres. $15.00.   96 Livres. $15.00.   Sequin. $2.20

SILVER.

20 Grani 15c.   2 Lire. 36c.   Teston. 28c.

Scudo. 97c.   Crown. 97c.   Scudo. 97c.

Five Francs. 93c.   Crown. 97c.

2 Carlins. 15c.   10 Grani. 7c.   2 Carlins. 15c.   Paul. 9c.   20 Grani. 15c.

ITALIAN STATES.

SILVER.

Scudo 93c.

Five Paul. 45c.

Scudo. 93c.

Scudo. 86c.

Scudo. 93.

Half Scudo. 45c.

Scudo. 93c.

Scudo. 93c.

Scudo. 86c.

Scudo 93c.

Scudo. 93c.

Scudo. 86c.

ITALIAN STATES.

SILVER

Silver Lion. $1 00.   Flor   27c.

Ten Pauls. 97c.   Testoon. 28c.   Ten Pauls. 97c.

Florin. 27c.   Crown. 97c.   Scudo. 93c.

10 Soldi. 8c.   ½ Lira. 8c.   5 Soldi. 4c.   10 Soldi. 8c.   10 Soldi. 8c.

SWITZERLAND. (SILVER)

½ Florin. 20c.   Crown. 80c.

Half Crown. 40c.   Crown. 80c.

Crown. 80c.   Half Crown 40c.   Crown. 80c.

Quarter Crown 20c.   Five Batzen. 9c.

Five Batzen. 9c.   Two Francs. 3?c.

HOLLAND. (GOLD.)

Five Guilders. $1.98.   Ten Guilders. $3.99.

Ten Guilders. $3.99.

SILVER.

Guilder. 35c.

2½ Guilders. 96c.

3 Guilders. $1.20.

8 Stivers. 7c.

Ducatoon. 98c.

Guilder 35c.

Rix Dollar. 98c.

3 Giulders $1.08.

5c.

25 centimes 5c.

¼ Guilder 8c.

Two Stivers. 3c.

BELGIUM, DENMARK & HOLLAND.
SILVER.

Rix Dollar. 93c.

Ten Stivers. 18c.

Rix Dollar. 93c.

Rix Dollar. 93c.

Ten Stivers. 18c.

Three Guilders. $1.08.

6 Stivers. 9c.

10 Cents. 4c.

2 Skillings. 1c.

6 Stivers. 9c.

Ten Ore. 2c.

Twenty-five Ore. 6c.

Krone. 26c.

Two Kroner. 52c.

THE COIN CHART MANUAL.
PLATE XLI.

DENMARK & HOLLAND. (GOLD.)

Ducat. $2.20.
SILVER.

Ducat. $2.20.

Rigsdaler. $1.08.

Six Stivers. 9c.

10 Skillings. 2c.

20 Skillings. 5c.

Ducatoon. 93c.

12 Skillings. 4c.

Rix Dollar. 93c.

30 Stivers. 57c.

30 Stivers. 57c.

Guilder. 35c.

NORWAY AND SWEDEN. (GOLD.)

20 Kronor. $5.34.

Ducat. $2.20.

SILVER.

Specie Dollar. $1.10.

Specie Dollar. $1.10.

1-6 Dollar. 16c.

Dollar. $1.02.

40 Schillings. 62c.

60 Schillings. $1.00.

Specie Dollar. $1.00.

12 Skillings. 5c.

4 Skillings. 1c.

⅟₁₆ Dollar. 5c.

Krone. 26c.

RUSSIA AND POLAND.

GOLD.

PLATINA.

5 Rubles. $3.90.   5 Rubles. $3.90.   Six Rubles $4.60.

SILVER.

5 Kopecs. 3c.

10 Kopecs. 6c.

Ruble. 73c.   10 Kopecs. 6c.   1½ Ruble. $1.07.

Ruble. 73c.   Ruble. 73c.   Ruble. 73c.

20 Kopecs. 14c.   15 Kopecs. 10c.   5 Kopecs. 3c.   5 Kopecs. 3c.

Half Ruble. 36c.   Quarter Ruble. 18c.

POLAND.
SILVER.

Five Zlot. 53c.   Three Zlot. 16c.

GREECE.
GOLD.

Twenty Drachms. $3.44

SILVER.

Half Drachm. 8c.

Five Drachma. 15c.   Five Drachma. 95c.

TURKEY.

GOLD.

10 Piastres. 43c.

SILVER

Piastre. 4c.   Two Piastres. 8c.

Twenty Piastres. 87c.

INDIAN STATES.

GOLD.

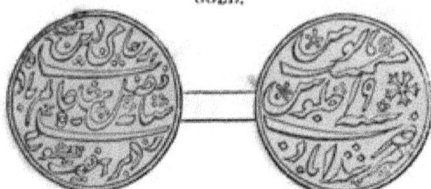

Mohur. $7.10.

SILVER.

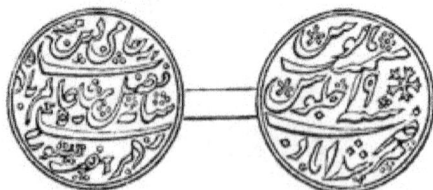

1¼ Pagoda. 35c.

Rupee. 45c.

¼ Rupee. 10c.

Half Rupee. 22c.

¼ Rupee. 10c.

HAITI.

BASE SILVER.

25 Centimes.

100 Centimes.

12½ Centimes.

THE COIN CHART MANUAL.
PLATE XLVII.

BELGIUM.

GOLD.

Twenty-five Francs. $4.72.

Twenty Francs. $3.86.

SILVER.

Five Francs. 96c.

Five Francs. 96c.

CENTRAL AND SOUTH AMERICA.
SILVER.

Peso. 90c.

Half Peso. 38c.

Two Reals. 20c.   Two Reals. 20c.   Two Reals. 20c.

Four Reals. 40c.   Two Reals. 20c.   Two Reals. 20c.   Two Reals. 20c.

GERMAN EMPIRE.
GOLD.

Twenty Marks. $4.76.   Ten Marks. $2.38.

SILVER.

Twenty Pfennig.   4c.   Fifty Pfennig.   11c.

One Mark.   23c.   Two Marks.   46c.

Five Marks. $1.19.   Five Marks. $1.19.

Five Marks. $1.19.   Five Marks. $1.19.   Five Marks. $1.19.

JAPAN.

GOLD.

Value varies greatly.

One Yen. 99c.

Two Yen. $1.98.

Five Yen. $4.98.

Twenty Yen. $19.94.

SILVER.

Itzbu. 33c.

Five Sen. 4c.   Ten Sen. 9c.

Twenty Sen. 19c.   Fifty Sen, 49c.

JAPAN.

SILVER.

One Yen. $1.00.　　　　　　　　One Yen. $1.00.

One Yen. $1.00.　　　　　One Yen. $1.00.

SWITZERLAND.

SILVER.

Two Francs. 8c.

Five Francs. 9c.

GREAT BRITAIN.

SILVER.

Crown. $1.15.

Crown. $1.15.

Shilling. 23c.   Shilling. 23c.

Crown. $1.15.

MISCELLANEOUS.

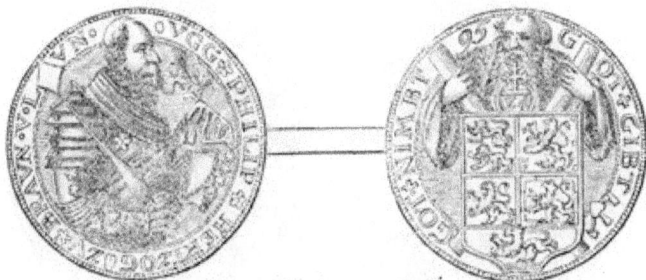

Brunswick, Crown. $1.02.

Denmark, Crown. $1.06.

Norway, Crown. $1.05.

Switzerland, Crown. $1.02.

MISCELLANEOUS.

Russia, Gold, Double Imperial. $15.75.

Portugal, Gold Crusado. $16.00.

Spain, Crown. $1.00.

Egypt, 10 Piastres. 43c.

Hamburg, Crown. $1.00.

MISCELLANEOUS.

Sweden, Crown. $1.10.

Parma, Scudo.   97c.

Sedan, Crown. $1.06.

Mexico. Gold. 20 pesos. $19.67.   Hamburg, 5 Marks, $1.19.

STANDARD COIN CATALOGUES,

Published by J. W. SCOTT & CO., 146 Fulton Street,

NEW YORK CITY.

☞ SPECIMEN PAGES REDUCED TO ONE QUARTER SIZE.

COPPER COINS.

Massachusetts Half Cent, 1787-8, .. from $1.00 to $8.00
"   Cent, "   .. "   33 - 1.00

New Jersey Cent, 1786 .. .. from $ 50 to 1.25
"   "   1787 .. "   10 - 50
"   "   1788 .. "   25 - 1.00
"   "   For Type, .. "   1.50 - 8.00
"   "   Head to Left, .. "   8.00 - 6.00

Connecticut Cent, 1785 .. from $ 53 to 1.60
"   "   1786 .. "   25 - 50
"   "   1787 .. "   10 - 30
"   "   1788 .. "   25 - 50

Vermont Cent, 1785 .. .. from $1.50 to $8.00
"   "   1786 .. .. "   1.00 - 8.00

SILVER COINS

2

United States Silver Dollars.

1794 Flowing Hair, ... $ 425.00 $75.00
1795 " 2.00 1.50

1795 Fillet Head, 2.00 2.50 3.00
1796 "   2.50 2.50 2.50
1797 "   4.00 2.50 8.00

1798 Fillet Head, Small Eagle, Large Eagle, 2.00 2.00 1.75
1799 "   2.00 1.75 1.50
1800 "   2.00 1.60 1.60
1801 "   2.00 1.60 1.60
1802 "   2.50 1.60 1.50
1803 "   2.50 2.00 1.75
1804 "   Extremely rare.

AMERICAN & FOREIGN COPPER COINS.

This catalogue gives the selling price of the various series of coins of which it treats, the text being profusely illustrated with engravings of the rarer pieces, to enable the collector to determine their nationality and date of issue. The value of the American coins is given in three degrees of preservation, which will be found a valuable feature of the work.

It will be found of great value to all Newsdealers and Storekeepers, as it gives the fictitious value of all American copper. By its means many small traders have made hundreds of dollars by selling coins taken in their stores, which they would otherwise have passed out in change. Price 25 cents, post free.

AMERICAN & FOREIGN SILVER COINS.

This handy manual is gotten up in the same style as the Copper coin catalogue, and is illustrated with well-executed engravings, of every American silver coin ever issued, and some of the most interesting foreign ones

Our remarks concerning the value of the Copper coin catalogue, will apply with still greater force to this, for as the silver coin which has been hoarded up for the last fifteen years, comes again into circulation, many rare and valuable pieces are sure to reward those, who take the time to look at the dates, before paying them away. It must not be thought that it is only the old pieces that are valuable, as, for instance, the publisher will pay $5.00 for the silver dollar of 1854, and so with other comparatively recent dates.

Price 25 cents, post free. Or the two bound in one volume, with a supplement containing fac-similes, of a number of old Roman and Greek coins. Price 50 cents, post free.

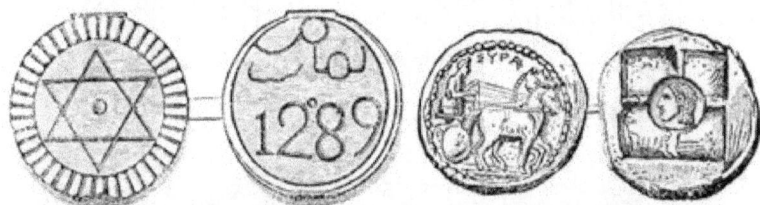

New Publications,

MAY, 1879.

Messrs. SCOTT & COMPANY

Take great pleasure in announcing to the public that they have issued this day a work of great value to all interested in the history of their country, entitled

"Colonial Continental Confederate Currency,

" *Their present market value.*

" *To which is added a complete Price List of*

U. S. Fractional Currency.

Price - - - - 50 Cents.

It would be impossible at this date to claim that the list is perfect, but great care has been taken in its preparation, and every known variety of all the different kinds of paper money which have circulated in this country, has been tabulated according to date, so that any note is easily found, while the numerous full sized illustrations of Colonial and Continental money give material aid, likewise add interest to the book for the general reader. As an instance of its completeness we may call attention to the fact that 74 pieces of U. S. Fractional Currency are catalogued, while the highest number heretofore chronicled was only 48.

Besides being valuable as a check list of all uncurrent money issued by authority in this country, it is a comprehensive price list of Messrs. Scott & Company's large stock, the prices of which have been placed as low as the great and increasing demand for these interesting mementoes of our country's struggles for existence will admit of.